BE THE CHANGE in your School

Shannon Welbourn

Crabtree Publishing Company
www.crabtreebooks.com

Dedicated by Shannon Welbourn

For Dakota, who always inspires change.

Author
Shannon Welbourn

Publishing plan research and development
Reagan Miller

Editor
Anastasia Suen

Proofreader and indexer
Wendy Scavuzzo

Design
Samara Parent

Photo research
Samara Parent

**Production coordinator
and prepress technician**
Samara Parent

Print coordinator
Katherine Berti

Photographs
Alamy: Myrleen Pearson (front cover)
Thinkstock: p. 16
The Be One Project: p. 8-9
istockphoto: p. 6
Shutterstock: Anna Baburkina: p. 7 (top right);
    Elenarts: p. 5; Krailurk Warasup: p. 7 (middle)

All other images by Shutterstock

Library and Archives Canada Cataloguing in Publication

Welbourn, Shannon, author
    Be the change in your school / Shannon Welbourn.

(Be the change)
Includes index.
Issued in print and electronic formats.
ISBN 978-0-7787-0626-7 (bound).--ISBN 978-0-7787-0638-0 (pbk.).--
ISBN 978-1-4271-7611-0 (pdf).--ISBN 978-1-4271-7607-3 (html)

    1. Schools--Juvenile literature. I. Title.

LB1556.W45 2014   j371   C2014-903842-9
                                       C2014-903843-7

Library of Congress Cataloging-in-Publication Data

Welbourn, Shannon.
  Be the change! : be the change in your school / Shannon Welbourn.
     pages cm. -- (Be the change!)
  Includes index.
  ISBN 978-0-7787-0626-7 (reinforced library binding) -- ISBN 978-0-7787-0638-0 (pbk.)
  -- ISBN 978-1-4271-7611-0 (electronic pdf) -- ISBN 978-1-4271-7607-3 (electronic html)
  1. Schools--Juvenile literature. 2. School environment--Juvenile literature.
  3. Educational change--Juvenile literature. 4. Young volunteers--Juvenile literature.
  5. Social action--Juvenile literature. I. Title.
  LB1556.W45 2015
  371.01--dc23
                                       2014032611

Crabtree Publishing Company

Printed in Canada/102014/EF20140925

www.crabtreebooks.com   1-800-387-7650

Published in Canada
Crabtree Publishing
616 Welland Ave.
St. Catharines, Ontario
L2M 5V6

Published in the United States
Crabtree Publishing
PMB 59051
350 Fifth Avenue, 59th Floor
New York, New York 10118

Published in the United Kingdom
Crabtree Publishing
Maritime House
Basin Road North, Hove
BN41 1WR

Published in Australia
Crabtree Publishing
3 Charles Street
Coburg North
VIC 3058

Contents

Be the change

Gandhi was a great leader who **inspired** change around the world. He believed "we must be the change we wish to see in the world." This is how he lived his life over 100 years ago. Gandhi was **selfless**. He put others before himself. Gandhi showed us one person's belief can start **positive action**.

*Gandhi lived in India. His **compassion** for change was felt around the world.*

Canada

U.S.A.

India

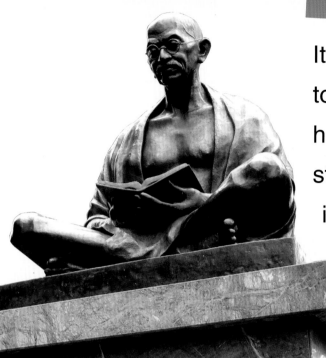

It takes hard work and courage to be the change. But everyone has the power to do it. You can stand up for things you believe in. You can change things you feel are not right. You can take positive action.

"MA VIE EST MON MESSAGE"

"MY LIFE IS MY MESSAGE"

MAHATMA GANDHI
(1869 - 1948)

OFFERT À LA VILLE DE GENÈVE
PAR LA RÉPUBLIQUE DE L'INDE EN 2007

*Gandhi left a **legacy** from the way he lived his life.*

MAKING CHANGE HAPPEN!

What does it mean to "be the change?"

Making a change at school

You can share Gandhi's belief. Live his message in your everyday life. How can you make positive changes? Think about your **school community**. Your school community includes the playground, building, and all your classmates and teachers.

The neighborhoods around the school are also part of your community.

You spend a lot of time at your school. Help to make it the best place it can be. Think about the things in your school that matter to you.

MAKING CHANGE HAPPEN!

Imagine your dream school...
What is it like?
How do people treat each other?
What activities are offered?
How does it feel to be in this school?
Think of ways to make your school more like your dream school.

Change in action

There are many ways to make positive changes at your school. Matthew Kaplan is one person who made his school a better place.

iDEA

NAME:
Matthew Kaplan

FROM:
Phoenix, Arizona

CAUSE:
Prevent bullying in schools

At the Radio Disney Music Awards, Matthew was honored with the Hero for Change award.

The Be O.N.E. Project

In his school, Matthew saw students being bullied. He knew all students should have a safe place to learn. He wanted to create a place where people could feel accepted. In 2011, Kaplan started the Be O.N.E. project when he was only 13. This

stands for Be Open to New Experiences. The goal of the project is to prevent bullying. The project started small. Matthew wanted to make things better at his school. Then, his brother was bullied on the computer. Matthew realized there was a greater need for support. Years later, Matthew continues his passion for change. His ideas are now used in schools across the United States.

Finding a need

Matthew was inspired by the experiences of students at his school. He found a way to change something important to him. What is important to you? Look in the school halls and classrooms. Look outside. Do you notice anything that could be improved?

Working together helps make your school a positive place for everyone.

Making a change

There are so many ways to get started. Talk to your friends. How would they improve the school? Brainstorm ideas together.

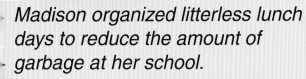

Madison organized litterless lunch days to reduce the amount of garbage at her school.

Olivia started a recycling program in her school.

James, Noah, and Jacob shoveled driveways in the community around their school.

MAKING CHANGE HAPPEN!

What is your idea for change?

Once you have found a need, you can inspire positive change.

Learning and preparing

Hannah saw a space outside that no one was using. She also noticed that many students did not have fresh fruits or vegetables for snacks. Hannah decided to start a gardening club to give students healthy snacks.

Join the Gardening Club!
- After lunch
- Outside in the schoolyard
- We can grow healthy snacks!
- Everyone welcome

Nathan is planting some seeds.

Hannah and Elliott are planting some seedlings.

Isabella waters the plants. Plants need water to grow.

MAKING
CHANGE
HAPPEN!

What did you find? What can you help change? After choosing a problem, investigate what you need to do to help. Think about who you will need to talk to. Maybe a teacher or principal can help you.

The carrots are growing.

Julia is picking some carrots.

Ethan's first bunch of carrots from the school garden.

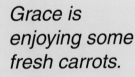

Grace is enjoying some fresh carrots.

Make an action plan

An **action plan** helps you know what needs to be done to make your change. Ask yourself:

What is the change I want to make? I want to start a new welcome club.

Who am I helping? New students

What can I do? I need to make an action plan.

Why is this important to me? Help new students coming to my school. No one likes to be alone at recess.

Who can help? Me!

MAKING CHANGE HAPPEN!

Do you know what change you want to make? Take your idea and plan how to make it work.

Andrew decided he wanted to start a welcome club. Use his outline to help you write your own action plan.

Decide what steps you need to put your plan in to action. Name your project. Ask people to help. Your idea for change is important. Be able to explain why. This will help others be inspired to help, too!

Andrew's Welcome Club Action Plan

What are my goals?
I want kids to feel welcome in my school. Moving and switching schools can be hard. The Welcome Club can help.

What specific service will I provide?
Show new students around the school.

How will I provide this service?
Help them find classrooms, restrooms, gym. Anywhere they are going in the school. Include **accessible** options.

Who will perform the service?
Myself or anyone who wants to help. Kids of same age can help welcome new students. They can start making friends right away.

When and where will this happen?
Anytime. Whenever it is needed.

What supplies will I need?
Make a welcome bag. Fill it with goodies for the new student. Talk to teachers for ideas about items they ask their students to have. Include a school map. Mark emergency exits.

15

Do it!

You have worked hard on your action plan for change. Now it is time to do it!

Principal Samuels talked to Andrew. A new student was starting at their school. Andrew got to work.

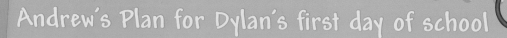

Andrew's Plan for Dylan's first day of school

8:45 AM
- Meet Dylan at front entrance of school
- Show Dylan the way to Mrs. Taylor's grade three class
- Help him find a hook for his backpack
- Show Dylan to his desk

8:55 AM
- School day begins

10:35 AM
- Recess
- Show Dylan where restrooms are located
- Go outside, swing, play basketball, meet other students

11:15 AM
- Back to class with Mrs. Taylor

12:55 PM
- Lunch
- Eat at desk
- Play outside after eating lunch

1:35 PM
- Back to class with Mrs. Taylor

3:15 PM
- Dismissal
- Make plans to see Dylan again tomorrow

16

Don't give up!

It may take others time to accept your idea. They may find it difficult to change something they are used to. Don't give up.

Remind yourself why this change is important. Remember, everyone faces challenges. It is important to stay true to your beliefs. Don't be discouraged.

Share it! Celebrate it!

Share your ideas with other students. This will help your idea grow. Your change can help more people than you imagined. Others may also be encouraged to take action. Keep notes. Track the change over time. Hannah took pictures as her garden grew. Your change might happen quickly. It might take time to catch on. Either way, write down what you do for your project. Keep track of what works and what might need to be changed next time.

You can give a presentation about your project to your class.

Be proud of yourself

Be proud of the change you made. Recognize people who have helped you. Who has helped in your vision for success? People will notice your positive energy. They will want to be a part of the new change. You may even inspire others. More things can be better at your school.

Think about it!

You did it! Think about your changes in your school. This will help you continue positive action. Maybe the change is ongoing. Maybe the change will take place over time. Some changes can only be done in small parts. Maybe you want to make things even better.

Think about it:

- Who did you help?

- How did helping make you feel?

- What did you learn? What did you not know before?

- What new questions or ideas do you have?

- Is there anything you would do differently next time?

Keep being the change

Every day you can think of ways to be the change. Your changes can be big or small. They can happen right away. You can continue to make your school better—even after you have graduated!

MAKING

CHANGE

HAPPEN!

How will you make sure your change continues? How can it grow even when you have left the school?

Helping others helps you

Something happens when you help others. You feel good about how you helped. You will boost your confidence. Others will be proud of you. Thinking of ways to help others is rewarding. You could make new friends. You may learn to do or try something new. Believe in your ability to make positive changes at school. The possibilities are endless!

You can be the change anywhere—at home, school, in your community, even the world!

Learning more

Websites

www.pencilsofpromise.org
An organization that builds schools, trains teachers, and funds scholarships.

www.aworldatschool.org
Organization promotes every child's basic right to go to school and be allowed to learn.

www.pagesforpeace.org
Fifth grade students and their teacher creating the biggest book about world peace.

www.kidscanmakeadifference.org/what-kids-can-do
This website includes ideas of what kids can do to make a difference.

Volunteer organizations

www.ladybugfoundation.ca
The Ladybug Foundation raises money to help with homelessness projects in Canada.

www.metowe.com
Me to We offers leadership programs for schools, and Youth and School volunteering trips.

www.kidsareheroes.org
This organization shares humanitarian efforts to inspire young people to volunteer.

Books

Lee, Spike & Tonya Lewis Lee. *Giant Steps to the World*. Simon & Schuster, 2011

Becker, Suzy. *Kids Make It Better: A Write-in, Draw-in Journal*.
Workman Publishing Company, 2010

Wilson, Janet. *Our Rights: How Kids Are Changing the World*. Second Story Press, 2013

Words to know

Note: Some **boldfaced** words are defined where they appear in the book.

accessible (ak-SES-uh-buhl) adjective Capable of being used by people with disabilities

challenge (CHAL-inj) noun Something that needs a lot of skill, energy, and determination to deal with

compassion (kuhm-PASH-uhn) noun Feeling concern for another

inspire (in-SPAHYUHR) verb To encourage or guide someone

investigate (in-VES-ti-geyt) verb Find out about or get more information about something

legacy (LEG-uh-see) noun The impact someone's thoughts and beliefs have on society after their death

positive action (POZ-i-tiv AK-shun) noun Doing something that is good

selfless (SELF-lis) adjective Having more concern for others than for yourself

A noun is a person, place, or thing. A verb is an action word that tells you what someone or something does. An adjective is a word that tells you what something is like.

Index